1178194.33

Whoopi Goldberg

JUNIOR · WORLD · BIOGRAPHIES

A Junior Black Americans of Achievement Book

Whoopi Goldberg

SANDOR KATZ

CHELSEA JUNIORS

a division of CHELSEA HOUSE PUBLISHERS

English-language words that are italicized in the text can be found in the glossary at the back of the book.

Chelsea House Publishers

EDITORIAL DIRECTOR   Richard Rennert
PRODUCTION MANAGER   Pamela Loos
PICTURE EDITOR   Judy Hasday
ART DIRECTOR   Sara Davis

Staff for WHOOPI GOLDBERG
SENIOR EDITOR   Jane Shumate
ASSOCIATE EDITOR   Therese De Angelis
EDITORIAL ASSISTANT   Kristine Brennan
DESIGNER   Alison Burnside
PICTURE RESEARCHER   Sandy Jones
COVER ILLUSTRATOR   Janet Hamlin

First Printing
1 3 5 7 9 8 6 4 2

Library of Congress Cataloging-in-Publication Data
Katz, Sandor.
    Whoopi Goldberg / Sandy Katz
      p. cm.— (Junior world biographies)
Includes bibliographical references and index.
Summary: Profiles the life and career of the versatile Academy Award-winning actress and comedian.
ISBN 0-7910-2396-6 (hc: alk. paper).
    0-7910-4450-5 (pb)
    1. Goldberg, Whoopi, 1950- —Juvenile literature. 2. Comedians—United States—Biography—Juvenile literature. 3. Afro-American comedians—United States—Biography—Juvenile literature. 4. Motion picture actors and actresses—United States—Biography—Juvenile literature. 5. Afro-American motion picture actors and actresses—United States—Biography—Juvenile Literature. [1. Goldberg, Whoopi, 1950- . 2. Comedians. 3. Actors and actresses. 4. Afro-Americans—Biography. 5. Women—Biography.] I. Title. II. Series.
PN2287.G578K38 1996   96-17829
791. 43'028'092—dc20   CIP
[B]   AC

Contents

"This is my long, luxurious blond hair," says Goldberg, *playing a little African-American girl in her first hit,* The Spook Show. *The young girl believes that blond hair, light skin, and blue eyes will make her happy.*

1

"People Who Inhabit My Body"

One evening in 1983 a man named Mike Nichols was sitting in a small theater at New York's Dance Theater Workshop. He was a director and *producer* of many popular movies and plays, and he was used to the much bigger theaters of Broadway. But he was taking time from his busy schedule to see an extraordinary new talent he had heard about: a young, struggling African-American actress named Whoopi Goldberg, who was appearing in a production called *The Spook Show*.

In most theater productions, the stage is transformed into an imaginary world with scenery and props. Instead, Nichols looked out at an empty stage. Onto it came a woman dressed in simple clothes. She was Whoopi Goldberg, and without even a costume or props but only the most basic of tools—her voice, her body, and her face—she magically transformed herself into first one character and then another.

One of Goldberg's characters was a man named Fontaine, a loud-mouthed drug addict and thief. Instead of presenting Fontaine as a monster—as drug addicts are often portrayed—Goldberg showed the audience Fontaine's sensitive nature. Fontaine told the audience about his trip to Europe, describing his airplane flight across the ocean in hilarious detail. He imitated the pilot, the stewardess, and even an overcooked string bean on the dinner tray. The audience roared with laughter.

But the show got serious when Fontaine told how, once his plane arrived in Amsterdam, he visited the museum that had been the hiding place of Anne Frank. She was a young Jewish girl who, with her family, spent two years during World War II hiding from the Nazis, who were trying to kill all the Jews. In telling the story, Fontaine described the tiny space where the Frank family hid. "They had 20 hours a day of non-movement," Fontaine said. "No noise. They sat with no sound."

Then Fontaine was silent. Mike Nichols and the rest of the audience sat breathless in the awkward silence, experiencing a small piece of Anne Frank's suffering. Finally, Fontaine broke the silence, telling the rest of Anne's story. She had written about her life of hiding in her diary, which was later published. After two years in hiding, Anne was discovered by the Nazis, arrested, and taken to a *concentration camp*, where she died.

In Anne's bedroom, Fontaine had seen an inscription: "In spite of everything, I still believe people are really good at heart." At first

Fontaine could not understand this, because Anne and millions of others had died at the hands of the Nazis. How could the Nazis be so brutal, Fontaine wondered, and still be good at heart? But then he learned that the quotation came from Anne Frank's diary and had been written just days before she and her family were found and arrested. "You know," said Fontaine to the audience, "no matter what you do to children, they're always able to still see some good in there, 'cause they've got that ability to see the light at the end of the tunnel."

By the time Fontaine said this, the audience could see the good in him, a drug addict and thief who generally would be considered dangerous or destructive. Despite all of Fontaine's problems, Goldberg made him a human being her audience could understand.

Then suddenly Fontaine was gone, and Goldberg's face, body, and voice transformed her into a new character. This time she was a 13-year-old California surfer girl. In a different voice, Goldberg's character (who had no name) told the story of meeting a boy on the beach, having sex for the first time with him, and becoming pregnant. She explained that she tried to tell her priest and the nuns at church that she was pregnant, but they wouldn't listen or help her. Then she described what happened when she told her mother:

> She runs upstairs into my room. She got my suitcase and packed all my stuff and like she brought it downstairs. She went into the basement, got a screwdriver, came upstairs, totally changed the lock on the door, you know. And like she opened the door and like handed me my suitcase and like totally threw me out. And I'm like, 'whoa.' OK, like you're really supposed to be like my best friend and like she couldn't hear me. She couldn't hear what I was saying.

Alone, pregnant, homeless, Goldberg's character did not know what to do. Having nowhere to go, how could she possibly care for a child? With no one else to turn to, she tried to

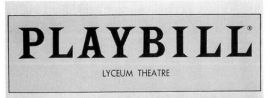

The Spook Show *was such a hit that it reopened on Broadway, and Goldberg was then called an overnight success. "It's tiring, being this overnight success that took ten years," she joked.*

give herself an *abortion*. Unfortunately she botched it, she explained at the end of her story, so now she would never be able to have children.

The surfer girl then disappeared as Goldberg again transformed herself. This time she did use a prop, but it was only a white shirt that she wore on her head, covering her long dark dreadlocks. "This is my long, luxurious blond hair," she said, now in the character of a young African-American girl. "I'm big for my age," she explained, "'cause we live near a nuclear reactor. My granny says we have to move soon or we're all gonna glow in the dark."

This little girl did not want to be black anymore. She told her mother she wanted to be white instead of black like her because her mother never did anything exciting, just worked all the time. But if she was white, she imagined, and had blond hair and blue eyes, then glamour and excitement would be hers. "Me and Barbie gonna live together with Ken and Skipper and Malibu Barbie," she fantasized, and she went on to explain that she wanted to go on the Love Boat (the cruise ship on the television show *The Love Boat*). "You need long hair to get on the Love Boat," she said. So Goldberg's character tried everything she could think of to change herself, even sitting in a tub full of bleach and burning her skin.

Goldberg then pulled the white shirt from her head and showed her real hair to the audience, saying, "It don't blow in the wind. It don't cascade down my back. . . . I want some other kind of hair to do something else." Spotting an African-American man in the audience, she asked, "You got hair like mine, huh?" When he acknowledged that he did, she said, "How come you don't have your shirt on? You came outside without it?" Then she looked around the audience and noticed many people with different types of skin and hair. "Nobody on TV looks like none of y'all," she said. Through this young character, Goldberg showed her audience how powerful television images can be. Instead of helping people accept themselves, these images may make us wish to be people we can never be.

Goldberg's final character was a woman with severe physical *disabilities* who was about to be married. To portray this character the actress twisted her body and strained her voice. "This isn't exactly a disco body," she joked.

14

Then she told the audience about a dream: "I used to dream that one day I was going to wake up and be able to move my hips and my legs. And my shoulder and my arm and my forearm and my wrist and my fingers. Move my neck and head. And I knew if I could do all that I could undoubtedly straighten out my vocal chords."

As she said these words, Goldberg's voice changed and became more relaxed. "Then I could be a normal person—able to do all the things that normal people do," she went on as she began a beautiful dance. "Like waving good-bye to two different people going off in two different directions at the same time, or exercising with Richard Simmons. To be able to go down the street without having people snicker or turn their heads or go 'tsk, tsk . . .' Just to be normal."

But then Goldberg's body began twisting and tightening again, and her voice became more strained. "But you know what happens when you wake up," she said. "It seems that you are the same exact person you were before you went to bed." Goldberg's character then told the audience about falling in love, despite her body, and she invited them to her wedding, a disco pool party. "Normal must be in the eye of the beholder," she concluded. She left the stage with this message of the worth of all human beings and the importance of loving who you are.

By the time the show ended, Mike Nichols, a longtime show-business professional who was not easily impressed, was *very* impressed. He could see that Whoopi Goldberg was an extremely talented performer. Her characters were so real that it was possible to forget the actress onstage and instead see and hear only the characters themselves.

Years later, in an interview for *Ebony* magazine, Goldberg said that she, too, forgot herself while performing these parts. "Those people who inhabit my body actually are full-blooded people. I just kind of sit back and watch what they're up to. I become part of the audience." This may be because Goldberg related so well to the struggles, fears, and frustrations of the characters she played. When she appeared in *The Spook Show* Goldberg was not yet 30 years old, but she had already been addicted to drugs, become pregnant as a teenager, been hurt and angered by racism, and been told that she had a disability. When Mike Nichols saw her perform *The Spook Show*, Goldberg was still almost unknown, struggling to support herself and her 10-year-old daughter.

After the show, Mike Nichols went backstage to meet Whoopi Goldberg. When he told her that he would like to produce her show on Broadway, she knew this was her big break. Broadway was the big-time theater, where Goldberg would be seen by more people, make more money, and find even greater opportunities. Whoopi Goldberg's answer to Mike Nichols that night was simple: "Yes! Yes!"

Carole Lombard fends off Lionel Barrymore in Twentieth Century. *As a child, Goldberg devoured films like this and learned to mimic the moves and expressions of the stars.*

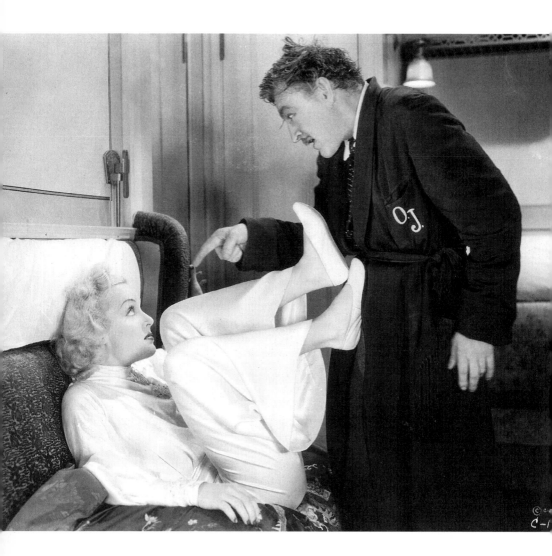

18

2

"I Could Be a Princess"

From the moment of her birth, Whoopi Goldberg was a performer. She was born Caryn Johnson in New York City on November 13, 1955. Her first act was to stick her thumb in her mouth while she was being born. In a 1991 *Vogue* magazine interview, Goldberg described the scene according to her mother, Emma Johnson: "Doctors were calling nurses to come over and look at this very odd baby who came out sort of ready to start. 'Let's party.'. . . My mom said she knew then that I was probably going to be an entertainer of some kind."

Caryn's father, Robert Johnson, left the family shortly after her birth. So Mrs. Johnson, who taught preschool in a program known as Head Start, raised Caryn and her six-year-old brother, Clyde, alone. Caryn grew up without ever knowing her father. Her mother, however, was a strong and responsible figure. "She could stop you from doing anything, through a closed door even, with a single look," explained Goldberg. "Without saying a word, she just has that power to, you know, rip out your tonsils." In contrast to her outspoken image today, Goldberg says that as a child she was "actually unassuming, very quiet. Kind of trying to stay out of everybody's way."

The Johnson family lived in a public housing project on 26th Street and 10th Avenue in Manhattan, in a neighborhood called Chelsea. "Chelsea was a neighborhood full of blacks, whites, Greeks, Jews, Puerto Ricans, and Italians," recalled Goldberg. She learned little bits of several different languages because, as she put it, "you had to be able to ask if your friend was home and if you could stay for dinner."

New York City was Caryn's playground. She recalls ice-skating in Central Park, watching the Thanksgiving Day Parade full of giant floats, and going to concerts, museums, the Hayden Planetarium, and Coney Island. New York City was full of adventure. But the biggest adventure for Caryn was watching movies, old ones especially, sometimes three or four in a single day. Watching these great actors was Caryn's earliest training in acting. "[D]uring the course of a day," Goldberg told an interviewer years later, "you would learn four or five ways to do any one thing. Today, I use the same technique; watch, absorb, and then give it back." Throughout her childhood she dreamed of acting in movies with her favorite stars of the 1930s and 1940s: "I had always planned to come and work with John Garfield and Carole Lombard," she said. "Because I knew I could do what they were doing, and no one had ever bothered to tell me they had been dead since before I was born."

When Caryn was eight, she asked her mother if she could be a princess. Mrs. Johnson answered that when a person is acting, she can be anything she imagines. So Caryn joined a theater program for young people at the Hudson Guild, a neighborhood community center. "I could be a princess, a teapot, a rabbit, anything," Goldberg remembers. Soon she was a star at the Hudson Guild. Her seventh- and eighth-grade teacher recalled that "acting was in her genes. She was a performer. . . . [and] played the lead in every play she was in."

As successful as she was at acting, however, Caryn was having a hard time keeping up at school. Years later the reason for this was discovered: Caryn had a learning disability called *dyslexia*, which causes a person to confuse the order of letters, making reading very difficult.

Dyslexia is quite common, though, and can be overcome if it is properly diagnosed. But Caryn's problem was not discovered until much later. As a young girl in school, she was considered "retarded," and she found this very hard to live with.

Another obstacle Caryn faced as a girl was racial *prejudice*. She grew up during the 1960s, when many African Americans were fighting for civil rights denied to them because of their race. In the Johnson household, Goldberg says, race was never an issue. Her mother would say, "Look, you're black. You woke up black this morning, you'll go to bed black tonight. But it doesn't make any difference."

But it seemed to make a difference in the world beyond the Johnson household, where Caryn sometimes experienced racial prejudice. As a teenager, she occasionally dated white boys. ("Why should I be worried about whether or

Drugs began luring many young people in the late 1960s and 1970s, and Goldberg was no exception. She became dependent on marijuana and LSD and dropped out of school. Here antidrug demonstrators march down New York's Sixth Avenue in 1970.

not a guy's white?" she asked many years later. "If he's an ax murderer, then I'm concerned.") But some prejudiced people do not approve of interracial dating, and Goldberg remembers that once she and a white date had eggs thrown at them.

Before her 17th birthday, the problems she was experiencing led Caryn to drop out of New York's Washington Irving High School. Without the daily routine, Caryn developed a drug problem and began to depend upon the marijuana and LSD that she—like many other teenagers at the time—had been experimenting with. Looking back on this period of her life, Goldberg says, "There ain't no joy in a high— none. You think there's a joy in a high because it feels good temporarily. But it feels good less and less often, so you've got to do it more and more often. It ain't your friend."

Caryn saw some of her friends' lives destroyed by drugs, and she eventually made the decision to quit. "I asked myself, am I going to keep doing drugs and kill myself, or figure out what I'm going to do with my life," Goldberg remembers. "I didn't stop altogether at once. It took many, many tries. You fall alot because it's hard." When she was 17, Caryn checked herself into Horizon House, a drug treatment program in New York.

Caryn was still not quite ready to make all the right choices for herself, however. At Horizon House she began dating her drug counselor. She married him when she was 18 because, she says, "it seemed like the thing to do." The marriage lasted less than two years. "You get married because you love someone and for no other reason," she later explained. "It can only last if you're deeply in love, and we weren't."

Although the marriage did not last, it left the young Caryn with a daughter, Alexandrea. Thus, before she was even 20, Caryn had struggled with a disability, dropped out of school, developed—and then overcome—a drug problem, married and divorced, and borne a child. For a while after her divorce, Caryn and her new baby moved in with her mother, Emma Johnson. But even though Caryn's life was far from organized, she still knew that she wanted to act. So in 1974, when a friend asked her if she and Alexandrea wanted to come to California, Caryn decided that she was ready to follow her dreams to Hollywood.

Goldberg played many different parts in her early days of acting with the San Diego Repertory Theater. Here she appears in Bertolt Brecht's play Mother Courage, *about a German woman's struggles during wartime.*

3

The Overnight Success (That Took 10 Years)

Caryn Johnson did not make it to Hollywood right away. To her disappointment, her cross-country journey landed her 100 miles south of Hollywood—in San Diego, California. Still, she was determined to pursue her dream and to continue developing her talents. So in San Diego Caryn joined a *repertory theater,* which is a type of theater in which the same group of actors and actresses work together in play after play. The San Diego Repertory Theater cast Caryn in many different roles—once in five different parts in *A Christmas Carol*. Sometimes she also performed routines as a stand-up comedian.

Caryn would gain valuable experience at the San Diego Repertory Theater; what she would not get was money. To support herself and her young daughter, she had looked for work as soon as she arrived in California. She held a variety of jobs, working as a bank teller, a bricklayer, and even as a beautician dressing the hair of dead bodies at a mortuary. "It's not a bad job," she told *People* magazine in 1984. "They can't talk back."

None of the jobs lasted, though, and Caryn and Alexandrea ended up on welfare. "I wasn't raised in a welfare household," recalled Goldberg, "so this was a tough thing to do." During this time of her life, Caryn was more concerned about surviving and feeding her daughter than about pursuing her acting career. "I didn't dream about [stardom]," Goldberg said later. "I dreamed about getting my kid more than one pair of shoes, or how to make $165 worth of groceries last all month." It took five years on welfare before she could support herself and Alexandrea. "The greatest thing I ever was able to do was give a welfare check back," Goldberg said. "I brought it back to the welfare department and said, 'Here. I don't need this anymore.'"

Caryn was still acting with the San Diego Repertory Theater, and now she also joined an *improvisational theater* group called Spontaneous Combustion. In improvisational theater actors don't follow a script. Instead, the audience gives them a situation, and the actors make up the action and dialogue from there. Caryn also befriended another actor, Don Victor, and became his partner. Together they did some late-night acting routines in comedy clubs.

It was in these early days of her acting career that Caryn Johnson became Whoopi Goldberg. A woman she acted with told her, "If

Goldberg in the 1988 film The Telephone. *She faced many difficulties during her early acting days, as she had a young daughter to support on her own. She made a living working odd-jobs that included hairdressing for a mortuary.*

I was your mother, I would have called you Whoopi, because when you're happy you make a sound like that practical joke whoopee cushion." For a while Caryn actually used the name Whoopi Cushion—until her mother convinced her that nobody would take her seriously with a name like that. Instead Emma Johnson suggested that Caryn use the last name Goldberg because some of her distant relatives might have been Goldbergs. Most people named Goldberg are Jewish, however, and Whoopi Goldberg is not. But she thinks her unusual name gives her an advantage with audiences. "Once they get past the fact that I'm Whoopi Goldberg, then they realize that anything is possible."

In 1980, Goldberg and her partner, Don Victor, were scheduled to perform in Berkeley, in northern California. Victor got sick at the last minute, though, and could not go. But Goldberg went anyway and performed alone, improvising three characters. "The audience went bananas," she remembers. "It freaked me out. I had never contemplated being a solo performer." A new stage of her career had begun.

Goldberg and Alexandrea moved to Berkeley, where Goldberg joined a well-known local theater group called the Blake Street Hawkeyes. With this group Goldberg developed the characters she performed in *The Spook Show*, which San Francisco audiences seemed to love. The group had a successful season in the area and then went on tour in the United States and Europe.

In 1983, the Blake Street Hawkeyes had an extended stay performing at the Dance Theater Workshop, a small experimental theater space in New York. By this time, Goldberg's *Spook Show* characters were a major part of the Hawkeyes' show. She was getting great reviews from critics, and people were coming to see *her*.

It was then that Goldberg was seen by Mike Nichols, the well-known producer and director. He was so impressed by Goldberg that he wanted to produce the *Spook Show* as a one-woman show on Broadway. Knowing that her life was finally changing, Goldberg said simply, "Yes! Yes!"

Renamed *Whoopi Goldberg*, the new version of *The Spook Show* opened in 1984 at the Lyceum Theater (only a mile or so from Goldberg's childhood home in Chelsea). Soon the show had become such a smash hit that it was taped and shown on cable television as an HBO special called *Whoopi Goldberg: Direct from Broadway*. Finally it was released as an album, too. It ultimately won a Grammy Award (the prizes given out in the recording industry) for Best Comedy Recording of 1985.

Suddenly Whoopi Goldberg was in the public spotlight. She seemed to have risen so quickly from being unknown to being a star that she was called an "overnight success." She objected to that description, though, because she had worked hard for years to develop her talent. "It's tiring, being this overnight success that took 10 years," she later joked. But it was true that literally overnight Goldberg was transformed from a struggling actress to a celebrity. Her picture was printed in newspapers and magazines, she was invited to appear on television talk shows, strangers recognized her on the street and asked for her autograph, and reporters wanted to interview her.

A reporter and a photographer from

People magazine visited her at home in northern California one day. They learned about her Mickey Mouse telephone and her cats, Lou and Bud, named after the famous 1940s film comedians Lou Abbott and Bud Costello. They found out that her favorite candy was Turkish taffy and that she wore a retainer at night to straighten her teeth. Goldberg even put in the retainer for a photograph, but her *press agent*, trying to protect Goldberg's image, screamed, "Not for the camera!!" For most stars, glamour is everything, whether or not it is genuine. "Why not?" asked Goldberg. "People should see it," she said. "It's real."

So Goldberg wore the retainer for the photographs, and people loved her because she was so real. Not everybody loved her, however: a critic for *Esquire* magazine wrote, "She'd better watch herself—or someday they'll be calling her Whoopsi." But most people now recognized her acting skills as extraordinary. In 1985, the University of Charleston, in West Virginia, gave

Goldberg—a high school dropout—an honorary university degree. "To experience Whoopi Goldberg," the degree read, "is to expand your mind, awaken your consciousness and view the world through new eyes."

And this was only the beginning.

Goldberg as Celie in Steven Spielberg's film The Color Purple. *Her moving portrayal of Celie earned Goldberg a nomination for an Academy Award for Best Actress—an award she did not win.*

4

"I Earned This"

One of the people who saw Whoopi Goldberg's show in New York was the filmmaker Steven Spielberg. He has made some of the most popular hits of all time, including *Jaws* and *E.T.* One day in March 1984, Goldberg answered the phone, and Steven Spielberg was on the line. "I'd like you to come and perform for me and a couple of friends," he said. Goldberg quickly agreed.

Spielberg's friends turned out to include singer Michael Jackson and musician/producer Quincy Jones. Goldberg knew she was in a new league as she sat among these superstars.

Goldberg performed *The Spook Show* for Spielberg and his friends. She also performed a short piece making fun of Spielberg's character E.T.—which he loved so much that he told Goldberg he wanted to cast her in a new movie he was directing called *The Color Purple*. "My teeth caught cold 'cause all I could do was grin," she recalled.

Goldberg already knew the story of *The Color Purple*, which was originally a novel by Alice Walker. It is about a young African-American woman named Celie, who lives in Georgia and who is badly mistreated first by her stepfather and then by her husband. Although she is uneducated and often frightened, she survives by keeping her sense of humor and hopefulness. Only when she meets and befriends another woman, Shug, does she develop the self-confidence and strength to become independent.

Goldberg had read Alice Walker's novel and had even written a letter to the author suggesting herself for a part in the movie. But Goldberg imagined herself in the role of Sofia, a strong and outspoken character with a small role. "I figured Sofia would be a nice little part, a nice little way for me to break into the movies."

Spielberg, however, had a different idea. Even though Goldberg had never acted in a film before, he wanted to take a chance and cast her in the starring role of Celie. Goldberg tells the story of how she had to be convinced by Spielberg not to want the smaller part: "When he said, 'No, first of all you're too small to play Sofia as we see her, and you're better suited to play Celie,' and this was all along Alice's idea, I kind of said, 'Oh, I don't know.' And then I realized that Steven Spielberg's sitting there trying to convince me to be in his movie. And it was like"—Goldberg slapped herself on the face—"'Wake up, stupid. Say yes.'"

Goldberg starred in *The Color Purple* and was a hit. A movie critic for *Rolling Stone* magazine wrote, "She says everything with her face, and her voice; not the words of the voice but its sound, and the mouth that speaks it." The critic continued, "In the picture's single best bit of acting, Goldberg simply watches Shug, one emotion after another bubbling to the surface of that face, each bursting the emotion that came before and then waiting to be contradicted by the next."

Goldberg was so extraordinary as Celie in *The Color Purple* that she was nominated for an Academy Award. The Academy Awards, also known as Oscars, are Hollywood's highest honors for the people who make the most popular and best movies each year. It is unusual for a first-time actor to be nominated for an award, but Goldberg's performance in *The Color Purple* earned her a nomination for 1985's Best Performance by an Actress in a Leading Role.

When the night of the awards ceremony arrived, Goldberg was very nervous. The most celebrated stars of Hollywood arrived at the

Academy Awards ceremony in limousines, dressed in glamorous outfits. The ceremony was televised all around the world, with millions of viewers.

Goldberg sat through hours of award presentations before it was time to announce the award for Best Actress. Finally, the moment arrived. Goldberg braced herself as she heard the words, "The envelope, please." She had dreamt of this moment since she was a young child. "And the winner is"—Goldberg was on the edge of her seat as she waited for the name of the winner—"Geraldine Page." Goldberg lost to an experienced Hollywood actress and went home disappointed.

But *The Color Purple* was only the beginning of Goldberg's film career, and it opened the doors of Hollywood to her. In the next few years Goldberg appeared in *Jumpin' Jack Flash* (1986), *Burglar* (1987), *Clara's Heart* (1988) and *The Telephone* (1988). Many critics found these films unimpressive. "In role after role," wrote *Time* magazine about Goldberg, "her acting was the best part of a succession of bad . . . films."

Goldberg, however, defended her choice of films and said she worked hard to get the parts she played. She even approached the studios herself and proposed roles. Otherwise, she said, she might only be asked to play prostitutes, abused women, and "mammies"—stereotypical roles black actresses have traditionally been limited to. To those who criticized her choices of film roles, Goldberg made a challenge: "If you want to see me in something better, write it!"

In 1990, Goldberg appeared in a movie called *Ghost*, about a man named Sam (played by Patrick Swayze), who is murdered and whose ghost wants desperately to contact his girlfriend, Molly (Demi Moore), to warn her that the murderer may attack her as well. In the film Goldberg plays Oda Mae Brown, who is a *medium*—a person who believes she has the power to communicate with the spirits of the dead.

Goldberg's performance as the eccentric medium Oda Mae Brown in Ghost *made it the most popular film of 1990. Oda Mae is the only person who can hear the ghost of recently murdered Sam (Patrick Swayze), who needs her to help him save his girlfriend before she too is murdered.*

At first, Goldberg's character is simply pretending to have these powers so people will pay her to "contact" their departed loved ones. But the ghost of Sam speaks to Oda Mae, and she is shocked to find herself genuinely hearing the voice of a spirit. She then becomes the hero

Goldberg arrives at the 1991 Academy Awards ceremony with Alexandrea. Although the actress admits that she was never really the "mommy type," she says she is proud of her daughter's independence.

of the film because she saves Molly's life by warning her about the murderer. Goldberg's performance in *Ghost* made it the most popular movie of the year and earned her another Academy Award nomination, this time for 1991's Best Performance by an Actress in a Supporting Role.

When the night of the Academy Awards ceremony arrived, Goldberg went to the theater with her daughter, Alexandrea. Goldberg had been nominated for an Oscar before and lost, so now she was especially nervous as she waited for the award to be announced. The winners are selected by members of the Academy of Motion Picture Arts and Sciences. The voting is secret, and the results are sealed in well-guarded envelopes, which are opened only on the night of the Academy Awards ceremony.

Finally the actor Denzel Washington stepped onto the stage to present the award for Best Supporting Actress. He named the five nominees and showed scenes from the films in which they had appeared. Then Washington said the magical words, "The envelope, please."

Goldberg could not believe it when she heard her name. She had won the Oscar! She was the first African-American woman to win an Academy Award in more than 50 years—the first since an actress named Hattie McDaniel won an Oscar for her role in *Gone with the Wind* in 1939.

Goldberg walked to the stage to accept

When Goldberg won the Academy Award in 1991 for her performance in Ghost, *she was so stunned that at first she could not speak. Later, she proudly told reporters, "I earned this."*

her award. But she was so shocked to have won that at first she was speechless. Looking out at the audience full of movie stars, Goldberg could not believe that some of her childhood heroes were there honoring her. "I looked around and saw all those people sitting there—Sophia Loren, Gregory Peck," she later recalled. "And then I just wanted to say 'Thank you' to them for being in all those movies I got to watch. For letting me come and play."

When Goldberg finally found her voice, she told the audience of stars and millions of television viewers that she had dreamed of this moment and had even practiced her acceptance speech since she was a little girl. "My brother's sitting out there," Goldberg joked, "saying 'Thank god, we don't have to listen to her any-more.'"

After the awards ceremony, Goldberg proudly and happily told reporters, "I earned this." From her childhood imitations of screen stars and throughout her years as a struggling actress, Goldberg had been working for this award her whole life. Now her dreams had come true. Whoopi Goldberg was a superstar.

After her success, Goldberg continued to make movies. Some have been serious dramatic

Goldberg as Delores Von Cartier teaches the nuns a few things in Sister Act, *a popular film that featured the actress in her first role as a singer.*

films, like *The Long Walk Home* (1990). This tells the story of the 1955 Montgomery bus boy-cott, one of the early struggles in the civil rights movement. In *Sarafina!* (1992), Goldberg plays a high school teacher in racially divided South

Africa, who inspires her students to fight for freedom. But most of Goldberg's films have been comedies, like *Sister Act* (1992). In this film, Goldberg plays a Las Vegas nightclub singer who witnesses a murder, reports it to the police, and then has to change identities so the murderers will not get her. Goldberg hides in a convent, pretending to be a nun. The wild, singing, cursing nightclub entertainer turns life in the convent upside down.

Producers began to view Whoopi Goldberg as a guaranteed box-office hit. When Disney paid her a reported $8 million to appear in *Sister Act 2*, she became "the first woman to break into the multi-million dollar boys' club," according to one Hollywood observer. Another commentator wrote, "This is the year that Whoopi Goldberg finally became bigger than her hair." In just a few years, Goldberg had climbed from being a struggling single mother on welfare to being the highest-paid woman in Hollywood.

Whoopi Goldberg was the first woman to host the Academy Awards ceremony, in 1994. Because of her strong opinions and sharp humor, many in the audience were nervous, but most judged the event a success.

5

Speaking Out

Whoopi Goldberg is famous not only for acting but also for speaking out on many controversial social issues. "I always thought the work of human beings was to watch out for each other," she says.

One important issue Goldberg has spoken out about is racism. Even as a star, she faces discrimination because, as an African American, she is still offered limited roles. "I'm fighting the label of 'Black' actress," Goldberg says, "simply because it's very limiting in people's eyes, especially people who are making movies. I don't want them to say, 'Oh, she's a Black actor, we can't use her.' I want them to say. 'Oh here's a great role. Call Meryl Streep. Call Diane Keaton. Call Whoopi Goldberg.'" Goldberg envisions a world where actors are not limited by the color of their skin. "The art of acting is not a black or white art," she says.

Goldberg has had some success at crossing color barriers. One of her roles, the part of Sarah in the film *Made in America* (1993), was originally written as a white character whose daughter discovers that the father she had thought long-dead is alive. "I'm a real good actress," said Goldberg in describing how she had wanted the part. "But look at me. I ain't white." Instead of rejecting her, though, director Richard Benjamin rethought the part and decided that making Sarah African American instead of white could produce a more interesting story.

Goldberg was also dealing with issues of

race when she made the film *Sarafina!* (1992). This is the story of a young girl and her teacher (Goldberg) in South Africa during one of the country's most turbulent periods. In 1992, Goldberg traveled to South Africa to film *Sarafina!* For many years, performing artists *boycotted*—or refused to go to—South Africa because black people there were being discriminated against under the country's racist system, called *apartheid*. Goldberg agreed to go for the filming only after the boycott had been called off by the African National Congress, the largest black political party in South Africa. She didn't know that some other black parties thought the boycott should continue. As *Newsweek* magazine wrote, Goldberg got "caught in the crossfire."

While Goldberg was in South Africa, she was publicly denounced by some of these political groups. Her passport (a crucial document for entering and exiting foreign countries) disappeared, and she suspected her political critics stole it. Yet Goldberg forgave these critics. "They needed some publicity," she reasoned, "so they used me."

Goldberg has used her own celebrity in much the same way—to gain publicity for causes she supports. She has worked to raise money for hurricane victims and for people with AIDS. A special concern of hers is homelessness. "It's disgusting that we could have this big, beautiful country and have families living in dumpsters," Goldberg has said.

To help the homeless, Goldberg—along with other comedians like Robin Williams and Billy Crystal—has worked for years on a project called *Comic Relief*. This is a comedy show (televised on HBO) that raises money to house and feed the homeless. Since the first *Comic Relief* show in 1986, it has raised many millions of dollars.

Another issue Goldberg has spoken out about is a woman's right to a legal abortion. She ended an unwanted pregnancy by abortion

Goldberg has used her success to help others. Here she serves homeless men Christmas Eve dinner at a soup kitchen in Washington, D.C., in 1987.

when she was a young woman, and she said it was a terrible experience. But still she strongly believes that a woman has the right to decide for herself whether to bear a child or end a pregnancy. "It is a decision that should be left to the people whose business it is to make it," she says. "And that's the individual—not the government, not the church." For Goldberg, the argument is not between supporting or opposing abortion.

It is between allowing or limiting individual rights.

This issue was close to home for Goldberg. She had borne her own daughter, Alexandrea, when she was only 18 and had raised her alone and without enough money. And when Alexandrea herself was 15, she

Another way Goldberg has found to help people has been by appearing in the show Comic Relief. *She and other comedians like Billy Crystal (left) and Robin Williams perform for free to raise millions of dollars that help the homeless. "It's not somebody else's problem," she says.*

became pregnant. Goldberg asked Alexandrea what she wanted to do, and her daughter responded that she had become pregnant because she wanted a baby. Although Goldberg reminded her that she did not have to continue the pregnancy, Alexandrea again said that her choice was to have a child. Goldberg did not think that this was the right decision but was glad that Alexandrea felt confident enough to make it.

Alexandrea's baby, Amarah, was born in 1990, and Goldberg posed with her daughter and new granddaughter in an ad for The Gap. Goldberg explained, "I wanted people to see that these things happen all over the world, all the time, and the only thing you can do is stand by your kids, whatever their decision is."

Not surprisingly, Goldberg's strong opinions on abortion rights and other important issues have sometimes angered people. When *The Spook Show* opened in San Diego in 1983, for example, anti-abortion activists picketed the theater because of Goldberg's pregnant surfer-girl character who gives herself an abortion. Goldberg didn't worry about the controversy, though. She thanked the picketers for bringing her show free publicity.

Indeed, over the years Goldberg has become known for speaking out and often getting into trouble. So when, in 1994, she was asked to host the Academy Awards ceremony—the first time a woman or an African American had hosted the extremely popular show—many people in the audience were nervous. But the first thing she said when she walked out on stage was, "So they went and gave me a live mike for three hours." She went on to tell the crowded auditorium and the millions of television viewers, "To make sure you don't feel shortchanged in the political soapbox department, I'm gonna get it all out of my system right now." She then listed a number of political causes: "Save the whales, save the spotted owl, men's rights,

women's rights, human rights, feed the homeless, more gun control . . ."

"I think I took care of everything," she
joked when she had finished. "Including my
career."

Goldberg with Vice President Al Gore on her 1993 late-night talk show.

6

Beyond Superstardom

Hollywood stardom was Whoopi Goldberg's biggest dream, but it was not her only dream. She was a great fan of *Star Trek: The Next Generation* and asked its producers if she could appear on the show. "They thought I was kidding," she recalled. Why, after all, would an Academy Award-winning movie actress, who could earn millions of dollars performing in a film, want to be paid much less to appear on television? Because she was a big fan, she told them simply. So they wrote her a part.

Goldberg appeared on the show from time to time as Guinan, who is from a planet where the life-forms are especially good at listening and understanding. Guinan is the *Enterprise*'s bartender, to whom the other characters confide their secrets. In 1992 Goldberg won an Emmy Award (the prizes given in the television industry) for Outstanding Actress for her performance in the series.

Goldberg appeared in other television series and even hosted her own talk show, called *The Whoopi Goldberg Show*. On it she interviewed entertainers and political and public figures ranging from Vice President Al Gore to *white supremacist* leader Thomas Metzger. White supremacists believe that white people are superior to those of other races. Goldberg was later asked why she had invited Metzger to appear on her show, and she admitted that she knew she would not be able to change his views. Still, she thought it was important to keep a dialogue going with racist people, because then "you can see where their hands are." If their racism was out in the open, she reasoned, it might be less dangerous. She even tried to joke about the difficult issue: when Metzger talked about his desire to separate the races, Goldberg said, "Where are you people going, 'cause I sure . . . ain't leaving."

One measure of Goldberg's stardom is the fact that on the night Bill Clinton was elected president, one of the first telephone calls he accepted was from her. Another measure is all the attention she gets. In 1994, when she married her third husband, Lyle Trachtenberg (a union organizer), helicopters with photographers and reporters hovered in the air over the wedding ceremony and made so much noise that none of the guests could hear anything. Goldberg could not stop laughing. "She would just about get hold of herself," reported a wedding guest. "Then she'd start up again. She

Claiming that she has always preserved her childlike wonder about the world, Goldberg in 1991 published Alice, *a modern fairy tale about a young black girl's adventures in New York. Actor LeVar Burton displays a copy of the book.*

tried to stop when she kissed Lyle, but she was still smirking." As Goldberg told her new husband, "This is what you're going to get with me."

As famous as Goldberg becomes, though, she has not lost sight of her priorities. She was voted kids' favorite actress three years in a row in a poll conducted by the Nickelodeon cable television network. Of her young fans Goldberg says, "They know I'm just as interested and as excited about the world and life as they are."

Goldberg loves entertaining young people so much that she has even written a book for children, called *Alice*, an updated version of Lewis Carroll's 1865 classic, *Alice's Adventures in Wonderland*. Alice is the story of a little girl who dreams of being rich: "She wanted big cars, diamonds, butlers with funny jackets, maids to cater to her every wish, and exciting, fun adventures—everything that money could buy." Hoping to get rich quickly, Alice entered every contest and sweepstakes she could. She wanted to win, and she was sure she would one day.

Every day Alice checked her mailbox, hoping to get a letter telling her she was a winner. One day she came home from school and found an envelope addressed to her. The letter read as follows:

Dear Winner,

Congrats on winning first prize in the Wegonnagetcha Sweepstakes. Your prize worth big bucks awaits you at 4444 Forty-fourth Street, New York, ground floor. And congrats again.

Signed,

The Wedungotcha Corp.

Alice decided to go to New York to claim her prize. She had never been to New York before, but she knew she could take a bus there. Her two best friends—her next-door neighbor, Robin, and her imaginary rabbit friend, Sal—

went with her.

Goldberg describes their big adventures in the wonderland of her own childhood in vivid detail: "There's something about being on a train in New York that's like nothing else in the world," she writes. "When the train is moving fast, the graffiti on other trains looks like the colors inside a kaleidoscope. There are all kinds of people, too, some reading, some staring into space, some staring at you. I could write a book about it but I won't because I'll bet you're wondering about Alice."

Alice and her friends had trouble finding 4444 Forty-fourth Street. Alice stopped a woman to ask for directions, and the woman—Mrs. Tu LowDown—invited her to a tea party and then chased her around trying to get her winning sweepstakes ticket. Alice got help from a fortune teller and finally found 4444 Forty-fourth Street.

But instead of earning her big bucks, the winning ticket was just a trick to get people into the office to try to sell them things. "They wanted me to give *them* money," Alice reported to her friends. "Since I wouldn't, they said I could have an electric can opener as a consolation prize . . . for $29.95."

Alice was disappointed. She wanted so very badly to be rich. But the fortune teller gave her something important to think about. "Dear, you *are* rich," she told Alice. "Look at your wonderful friends who stick by you whether you win or lose. Think about the wild adventure you've had. No amount of money could buy those things."

Whoopi Goldberg should know. She's had wild adventures, from her childhood of dreaming about the movies to her life as a Hollywood superstar. Goldberg struggled against a discouraging disability and against drugs; when she was still very young she worked hard for years to raise a daughter without enough money. But she believed in herself and never lost sight of what she wanted, developing her talent despite the obstacles. Now Goldberg has become a superstar, entertaining millions of people each year—and offering help and inspiration to those who face the same obstacles she has overcome.

Further Reading

Adams, Mary Agnes. *Whoopi Goldberg: From Street to Stardom.* New York: Maxwell Macmillan International, 1993.

Blue, Rose, and Connie J. Naden. *Whoopi Goldberg.* New York: Chelsea House Publishers, 1995.

Goldberg, Whoopi. *Alice.* Illustrated by John Rocco. New York: Bantam Books, 1992.

Hine, Darlene Clark, ed. *Black Women in America: An Historical Encyclopedia.* Vol. 1. Brooklyn, NY: Carlson Publishing, 1993.

"Lookout." *People Weekly.* May 28, 1984.

Martin, Linda, and Kerry Seagrave. *Women in Comedy.* New York: Citadel, 1986.

Riley, Dorothy Winbush, ed. *My Soul Looks Back, 'Less I Forget: A Collection of Quotations by People of Color.* New York: Harper Collins, 1995.

Chronology

1955	Caryn Johnson is born on November 13 in New York City
1964	Caryn joins the Hudson Guild, a young people's theater group
1972	Caryn drops out of high school; she undergoes treatment for drug addiction and marries her counselor
1973	Caryn gives birth to her daughter, Alexandrea
1974	She divorces and moves to San Diego, California, with her baby
1976	Caryn joins the San Diego Repertory Theater

1979	She joins the Spontaneous Combustion improvisational group and takes Whoopi Goldberg as her stage name
1980	Whoopi Goldberg moves with Alexandrea to Berkeley, where she joins the Blake Street Hawkeyes
1983	Goldberg is spotted by Mike Nichols, who offers to produce her one-woman show on Broadway
1984	Goldberg's show opens on Broadway; HBO broadcasts it as *Whoopi Goldberg: Direct from Broadway*; Steven Spielberg signs Goldberg to star in *The Color Purple*
1985	*Whoopi Goldberg: Direct from Broadway* wins a Grammy Award; Goldberg's performance in *The Color Purple* earns her an Academy Award nomination for Best Actress
1991	Goldberg wins the Academy Award for Best Supporting Actress for her performance in *Ghost*

1992	Goldberg wins an Emmy Award for her recurring role on *Star Trek: The Next Generation*; she publishes *Alice,* a children's book
1993	Whoopi Goldberg becomes the highest-paid woman in Hollywood; *The Whoopi Goldberg Show* airs
1994	Goldberg becomes the first African American and the first woman to host the Academy Awards ceremony
1996	Goldberg appears in *Eddie*

Glossary

abortion an operation performed to end a pregnancy

apartheid a policy of discrimination against non-European people in the Republic of South Africa

boycott to refuse to deal with or use the services of a person or an organization

concentration camp a camp where prisoners of war or refugees are kept, often under harsh conditions. Millions of Jews and other victims of the Nazis died in concentration camps during World War II

disability a condition that makes it difficult or impossible to perform tasks that most people take for granted

dyslexia a learning disability that makes reading difficult

improvisational theater a type of performance in which actors invent action and dialogue as they go instead of following a script

medium a person with the power to communicate with the dead

prejudice an attitude formed without knowing all of the facts, often directed against a particular race

76

press agent   a person employed to promote and protect the image of a celebrity or other public figure

producer   a person who finances the making of a theater, film, or television program

repertory theater   a company that uses the same group of actors and actresses in play after play

white supremacist   a person who believes that white people are superior to all others

Index

Sandor Katz grew up in New York City and attended Brown University, where he graduated with a bachelor's degree in history. He taught at alternative high schools in Providence, Rhode Island, and in Chicago, Illinois, before becoming the executive director of a community group in New York City. He then worked as a land-use planner and a senior policy analyst for AIDS for the New York City government. Katz's acts of political resistance include organizing protests against certain actions of the U.S. government in Central America and volunteering for the AIDS activist group ACTUP. He is the author of *Anne Frank: Voice of Hope* in Chelsea House's JUNIOR WORLD BIOGRAPHIES series, and his writing has also appeared in the *Nation* and *Outweek*.

Picture Credits